DATE DUE

The Ancient CHINESE

ROSEMARY REES

Heinemann Library
Chicago, Illinois

Customer Service 888-454-2279

Visit our website at www.heinemannlibrary.com

Design by Depke Design
Map illustrations by John Fleck
Color illustrations by Fred Anderson
Printed and bound in the United States by Lake Book Manufacturing, Inc.

06 05 04 03 02
10 9 8 7 6 5 4 3 2 1

Library of Congress Cataloging-in-Publication Data
Rees, Rosemary, 1942-
    The ancient Chinese : understanding people in the past / Rosemary
Rees.
        p. cm.
Includes index.
    ISBN: 1-58810-423-0 (HC), 1-4034-0097-0 (pbk.)
    1. China--Civilization--To 221 B.C.--Juvenile literature. I. Title.
    DS741.65 .R44 2002
    931--dc21
                                2001005325

Acknowledgments

The author and publisher are grateful to the following for permission to reproduce copyright
material:

Cover photograph courtesy of C. M. Dixon

Title page, pp. 21, 28, 45B, 51 Michael Holford; pp. 5T, 14, 36 C. M. Dixon; pp. 5B, 6, 18, 19B, 26, 30,
45T, 46, 52T, 55 Robert Harding Picture Library; pp. 7, 23B, 25, 27T, 32, 44, 50T Sally & Richard
Greenhill; p. 8 British Library/Werner Forman/Art Resource; pp. 9, 43 Freer Gallery of Art/The Art
Archive; p. 11 Trevor Page/Hutchison Picture Library; p. 12 Beijing Palace Museum/The Art Archive;
p. 13 Musée Cernuschi Paris/Photos12.com; pp. 15, 35 Bibliothèque Nationale, Paris/The Art Archive;
p. 16 Beijing Palace Museum/Werner Forman/Art Resource; pp. 17, 54T The British Museum; pp. 19T,
29, 34, 38, 58 Werner Forman/Art Resource; pp. 20, 42, 48 National Palace Museum, Taiwan/The Art
Archive; p. 23T MacQuitty Collection; p. 24 Musée Cernuschi Paris/Dagli Orti/The Art Archive; p. 31
Gerald Godfrey, Hong Kong/Werner Forman/Art Resource; p. 33 Lesley Nelson/Hutchison Picture
Library; pp. 37T, 57T The Art Archive; p. 39B Musée Guimet, Paris/The Art Archive; p. 40 Dave G.
Houser/Corbis; p. 41 British Library/The Art Archive; p. 47 Corbis Stock Market, London; p. 49 Ronald
Sheridan/Ancient Art & Architecture Collection; p. 53 Sovfoto/Eastfoto; p. 57B Art Gallery Of New
South Wales/Werner Forman/Art Resource; p.59 Michelle Jones/Ancient Art & Architecture Collection

Some words are shown in bold, **like this.** You can find out what they
mean by looking in the glossary.

Contents

Who Were the Ancient Chinese?

The ancient Chinese were people who lived thousands of years ago in the country we call China. They lived at first by hunting animals and gathering seeds and berries. Some of these people began following the herds of animals that roamed over the plains. They were **nomads,** who killed animals whenever they needed food. Other people settled down. By about 6000 B.C.E., they were living in villages along the banks of the Yellow River. They made pottery and farmed the **fertile** land using stone tools.

Around 3000 B.C.E., people started to mine copper, which they mixed with tin and lead to make **bronze.** The earliest known bronze objects in China date from 2300 B.C.E. The ancient Chinese also began to weave silk around the same time.

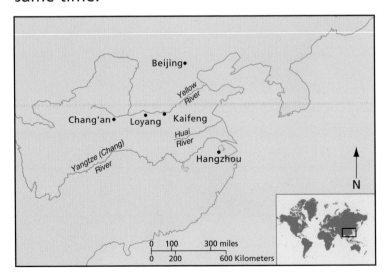

This map shows the Middle Kingdom, or Zhong-Guo. Foreigners called this land China.

4

Powerful families

The early settlers grouped together to protect themselves against enemies. Gradually, one family became more powerful than the rest and ruled over the others.

The Shang family, or **dynasty,** ruled from 1500 to 1122 B.C.E. The first towns and cities were built, a system of writing was invented, and bronze making became important.

The Chinese empire

In 221 B.C.E., the Ch'in dynasty, better known as Qin, conquered the land. Foreigners called the country China, but the ancient Chinese used a different name. They called their country Zhong-Guo, which means Middle Kingdom. They believed that their country was the center of the world. For many centuries, China led the world in inventions, ideas, and ways of government.

By 1227 C.E., a Mongol army led by Genghis Khan conquered north China. Later, in 1279, his grandson Kublai Khan ruled over all China. The Chinese took control of their country again in 1368.

This three-legged bronze bowl was made during the Shang dynasty. The ancient Chinese made many beautiful objects that still survive today.

This wine pot and warming bowl was made during the Song dynasty. It is made from **porcelain**, a very fine pottery. Large amounts of fine pottery and porcelain were made during this time.

5

How Do We Know About the Ancient Chinese?

Archaeologists study buildings and objects left behind by people in the past. They **excavate** different **sites** and create a picture of what life was like in the past.

Evidence from homes

Archaeologists found evidence of fires and stone tools in a cave at Zhoukoudian, near modern Beijing. Early humans, called Peking people, lived there in 450,000 B.C.E. By 28,000 B.C.E., *Homo sapiens* were living in another cave on the same site. Evidence shows they hunted animals, used stone tools, and gathered roots and berries for food.

Archaeologists found a village called Banpo in northwest China. People lived there around 5000 B.C.E. They were farmers. Their house walls were made from wood that had been split and woven together, and then spread with mud. This type of wall is called wattle-and-daub. The roofs were made from straw and supported by wooden posts. Outside the village was a pottery making area and a cemetery.

The first **emperor** of China, Qin Shi Huangdi, was buried with a life size army made from terra-cotta. Archaeologists excavated over 6,000 pottery soldiers in the 1970s. They have learned a lot about ancient Chinese armies from these soldiers.

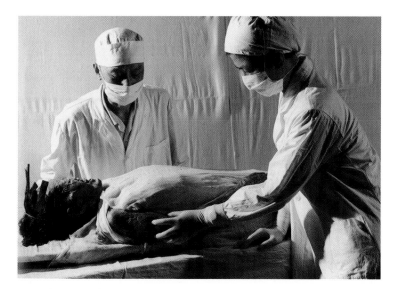

These medical workers are studying the body of a woman who died 2,100 years ago. Archaeologists can work out how old a person was when he or she died, what illnesses or accidents they suffered from, and their cause of death.

Evidence from tombs

By about 1500 B.C.E., important people were being buried in tombs. They were buried with food and many objects, called **artifacts,** they used in their everyday lives. Archaeologists can begin to understand about ancient technology by working out how these artifacts were made. Most of the food has rotted away, but archaeologists can find out what it was by studying the seeds and bones that are left.

Putting it all together

Archaeologists write down where everything is found. Finds from different sites are compared to see how people's ways of life changed and what may have caused the changes.

Evidence from Words and Pictures

Clues from writing

The ancient Chinese used sharp tools to write on bone and **bronze,** and ink to write on softer materials like **jade** and silk. They made small pictures, called **pictograms,** to represent each word or idea. This writing system is similar to that used by the Chinese today.

Oracle bones

Diviners used **oracle** bones to answer the king's questions about the future. They made cracks in flat bones, like the shoulder blades of an ox or sheep, and looked into the cracks to find the answer. They sometimes wrote the question and answer on the bone.

This is an oracle bone from China. People thought these bones were magical. They called them "dragon bones" and ground them up to make medicine. **Archaeologists** found out a lot about life in ancient China from the questions and answers written on the bones.

This painting shows Yang Guifei getting onto a horse. She was supposed to be one of the four most beautiful women in China. She lived during the Tang **dynasty.**

Ink writing

The ancient Chinese wrote on silk, jade, bamboo, and later on paper. They wrote stories, poems, books on medicine, and encyclopedias. There were also books about everything from how to make war to how to make clocks.

Clues from pictures

The ancient Chinese first painted pictures inside tombs. These pictures showed scenes from everyday life. They also painted pictures on silk banners that were buried with a dead person. These banners showed scenes from Chinese legends.

Later, they painted pictures of farming scenes and industry. Many pictures have survived, telling us what ancient Chinese technology was like at the time.

From Hunting to Farming

Hunting

The earliest people we know about in China lived there more than 500,000 years ago. The best known were called Peking people. They had stone tools, hunted animals, and gathered berries and roots to eat. Hunting and gathering continued in China until about 6000 B.C.E.

Farming

By 6000 B.C.E., the first farmers settled along the Yellow River. The river flooded often, which made the soil **fertile** and easy to work. These farmers built villages like Banpo that had about 500 people. They kept pigs, chickens, and dogs. They also grew a grain crop called **millet.**

This is a drawing of what Banpo might have looked like. The walls were made of wattle-and-daub and plastered on the inside. Some houses had plastered floors, but most were just dirt. Most houses had a fire pit that was used for cooking, heat, and light.

In hilly or dry land, fertile soil can be easily blown or washed away. Over hundreds of years, farmers have built terraces on their land to try to stop this from happening. These terraces are in the Guizhou **Province** in southern China.

Different farming, different cultures

China is so large that different areas have different climates. Thus farmers can grow different crops. Different climates and crops meant that ancient Chinese people developed different ways of life, or **cultures.** There were two distinct cultures in China between 5000 and 2500 B.C.E.

People of the Yangshao culture in western China (3950–1700 B.C.E.) grew millet and wheat. They bred silkworms and kept pigs and dogs. Their pottery was painted in red, black, or white geometric designs. The Longshan culture (2000–1850 B.C.E.) in northern China grew rice and millet, and kept pigs, sheep, goats, and cows. They made fine black pottery and were the first to write.

Government and Society

Kings and society

Kings ruled China until 221 B.C.E. The king owned all the land. Under him, **noble** families held large areas of land. In return, they agreed to protect the land from the king's enemies and fight for him when he asked them to. These noble families rented out some of their land to **peasants.** In return, the peasants agreed to work on the nobles' land and fight with him if the king needed men for his army. This way of paying with service instead of money to rent land is called a **feudal system.**

This picture was painted on a silk scroll during the Tang **dynasty,** about 1300 years ago.

This is a pottery model of a silk **merchant** on his camel. Foreign merchants came from all over the world to trade their gold for Chinese **porcelain** and silk.

Society in the Chinese empire

The emperor ruled over all China. Chinese society was divided into four groups:

1. The *Shi* were nobles and scholars;
2. The *Nong* were peasant farmers;
3. The *Gong* were craftworkers;
4. The *Shang* were **traders.**

The *Shang* were often very rich, while the *Nong* were often very poor. In ancient China, farming was more important than trading. So, the poorest farmer was more important than the richest trader or merchant.

Emperors and society

Qin Shi Huangdi came to power in 221 B.C.E. He was the first **emperor** of China and ruled over more land than any king before him. He changed the system of government because he wanted to control everything himself. He outlawed the feudal system, took power away from the nobles, and made the peasants pay taxes directly to him. He wanted his laws to be obeyed without question, and so he punished lawbreakers harshly.

The Mandate of Heaven

The Mandate of Heaven

The rulers of China believed that it was Heaven's wish that they ruled. This belief was called the **Mandate** of Heaven. Rulers kept the mandate if they were kind and fair. They also had to listen to their advisers, look after their people, and keep peace and order in the country.

Not all rulers followed the Mandate. Some were weak, greedy, cruel, or taxed the people so heavily that they starved. When this happened, the people rioted against their ruler. They said the ruler had lost the Mandate of Heaven and was not fit to rule. A new ruler then had the Mandate, and a new **dynasty** began.

This painting shows Chao Hsai, a good and wise governor. He felt sorry for the people and did not collect taxes from them. As a result, he lost his job.

Qin Shi Huangdi, the first emperor, wanted people to forget the old ways and ideas. He ordered books written in the past to be burned. Scholars whose ideas were in those books were buried alive. His plan did not work though. Many books were rewritten later.

The power of the emperor

The **emperor** had the power of life and death over his people. He could make people work for him. Qin Shi Huangdi made 700,000 people build his tomb.

The emperor's way of life

Emperors lived in palaces separate from their people. Government officials ran the country, under orders from the emperor. The emperor was then free to spend time as he wished.

Life in a Noble Family

At court

All the **emperors** were afraid that the **nobles** would get too powerful. So all the nobles had to spend some time at court. Then the emperor could find out if anyone was plotting against him.

At home in the town

Most noble families had a house in town. They were two or three stories high, with brightly painted walls. The roof tiles were decorated with imaginary creatures. Most houses had courtyards with goldfish ponds and potted plants. Some houses had trees and gardens. Inside, the houses had silk hangings on the walls, painted screens, and beautiful ornaments and objects.

Wealthy women had servants to do all the cooking and housework and to look after their children. When their husbands went to court, they went too. There they played games and listened to music.

At home in the country

The country homes of the nobles were just as grand as their houses in town. Because they were in the country, there was room for more gardens, trees, and pools. High walls surrounded homes. They had only one gateway that was usually guarded by soldiers. This was to keep the family safe.

Free time

Noble families did not work. Men and women wore silk robes with long flowing sleeves. They grew their fingernails very long, too. This was to show that they did not work. All their wealth came from their farms in the country. For fun, they held large banquets and watched dancers and acrobats perform.

Archaeologists have found pottery models in the graves of nobles. This model shows what a noble family's town house looked like. It has a gateway with two towers and the upper floors have balconies. This model was made 2,000 years ago during the Han dynasty.

Footbinding—"lily feet"

Around 970 C.E., rich Chinese families decided that small feet were more beautiful on a noble woman than normal-sized ones. When girls were very young, their feet were bent back and tightly bound. This broke the bones in the arch of the foot and turned the toes under. So, their feet grew to only half their normal length. Only women who had to work on the land did not have bound feet. As a result, many noble women could hardly walk. Footbinding was made illegal in 1926.

Mandarins and Warriors

By 2 C.E., there were over 59 million people living in China. The **emperor** ruled over everyone, but he could not govern everything by himself. He needed officials, or civil servants, to help him govern, and soldiers to protect him and defend his **empire** from enemies.

Mandarins and other officials

There were thousands of civil servants in ancient China. They were all men. The most important civil servants were the mandarins, who advised the emperor. They made sure people knew the laws and obeyed them, and they checked that everyone paid their taxes. Below the mandarins were ranks of lesser officials who ran everything, from building canals to collecting taxes to being judges.

These are two model soldiers from the terra-cotta army in the tomb of Qin Shi Huangdi. From these models we know that soldiers' weapons included knives, bows and arrows, axes, and spears.

This is the Grand Canal today. Over two million people were forced to build it. It was begun in 605 C.E. and was based on a more ancient canal system. The Grand Canal linked the Yangtze (now Chang) River with the Huai and Yellow Rivers.

Warriors

Any man over the age of fifteen could be forced to join the emperor's army, but not all of them were. This was because large armies were needed only when enemies threatened the empire.

Workers

For most of the time, men were more use to the empire working on their farms or as building workers. Most forced labor was done by Chinese convicts or prisoners of war. During the Han **dynasty,** every Chinese man had to work for the government for one month each year. They built dams, roads, flood barriers, hauled barges along the Grand Canal, and worked in salt and iron industries.

The government provided transportation for all mandarins and other important officials. Wherever they went, officials were treated with respect. Officials were not allowed to work in their own districts. This was in case they were tempted to do favors for their families and friends. This **bronze** model shows a mandarin sitting in his chariot.

Life in the Town

The first towns in ancient China were built close to the Yellow River during the Shang **dynasty.** Towns then grew over all the **empire.** These towns and cities were centers of **trade** and government and many were carefully planned.

Inside a walled town

A high wall surrounded each town and city. Inside, more walls divided the town into

This busy market scene is similar to the towns of ancient China.

separate areas, called wards. Each ward had its own entrance gate. Different groups of people lived and worked in each ward. They could go to other wards during the day, but had to return to their own ward at night. Rich people's homes had plenty of space, but in the poorer wards the houses were packed closely together.

What did the people do?

During the day, the streets were full of people. Farmers and **peasants** from the countryside brought their pigs, geese, fruit, and vegetables to sell at the market. There were stalls selling cooked meats, **jade** and **bronze** carvings, soup, baskets, silk, pots, and pans. Some people mended wheels or made harnesses, while others offered to cut hair, write letters, or tell fortunes. The poorest people begged for money and food.

All this activity took place on streets that were not paved. On dry days, the streets were dusty and on wet days, muddy. Piles of rotting garbage, manure, and lack of proper drains meant that towns were smelly places where disease spread rapidly.

Street entertainment was very popular in ancient Chinese towns. Acrobats and musicians performed in the streets and marketplaces. Performers also used animals in their acts, too.

Life in the Country

Most farms in ancient China were small, but there was usually enough work to keep one family busy all day. They usually managed to grow enough food to survive and pay their taxes to the **emperor.** However, if there were floods, war, or a drought, there might be no harvest on some farms. Then the family would have to choose between starving or selling their land and going to work for someone else.

A farmer's year in north China

In cold and dry northern China 2,000 years ago, the people grew mostly wheat and **millet.** In the spring, farmers plowed their land. Rich farmers used ox-drawn plows with iron-tipped blades that cut deep into the soil. Poor farmers pushed wooden plows through the soil. They sowed seeds by hand for wheat, millet, vegetables, and **hemp.** In the summer, they weeded and hoed the ground. They watered the crops in dry weather. In the autumn, if all went well, the crops were harvested. The farmers separated the wheat and millet seeds from the stems with wooden **flails.**

A rice farmer's year

Farmers grew rice in southern China, where winters were short and summers hot. In spring, they flooded the fields and plowed them so they turned into soft mud. In May, farmers planted rice seedlings by hand into the mud. They kept the fields wet for the rice to grow. When the rice was ripe, the fields were drained and the rice quickly harvested. Where two crops would grow in a year, the fields were flooded and ploughed again for more seedlings.

This stone carving shows a two story farmhouse with a tiled roof. Wealthy farmers often had two story houses.

Part of the farmers' crop was sent away to pay his taxes to the emperor. The rest was stored in **granaries.** They were built on stilts to keep rats and mice out. Some granaries had a dog kennel, too. Perhaps the dog was meant to frighten rats, mice, and thieves.

In wintertime, not much work could be done in the fields. Farming families spent the winter looking after their animals, mending their tools, and making clothes.

Today, people in China plant rice in the same way it has been planted for thousands of years.

Food and Cooking

When people in ancient China settled, their diet changed. They started to farm the land and grow grain, fruit, and vegetables. They could produce more food by **cultivating** the fields and growing crops than by raising cows and sheep to eat. This meant that there was little meat, milk, butter, or cheese in the ordinary Chinese diet.

Different foods

In the north, people ate **millet** and wheat. Sometimes the wheat was ground into flour to make noodles. In the north and south, people ate rice. Ancient Chinese people ate vegetables such as onions, Chinese cabbage, bamboo shoots, ginger, and lotus roots. They ate fruit such as melons, peaches, apricots, and orange berries called persimmons.

Poor people sometimes ate a little meat, mainly from chickens, ducks, and pigs. They ate fish and locusts, too. Rich people ate meat more often. They ate bears' paws, tiger and deer meat, quail, and pheasant. The fish they ate included crabs, shrimps, and clams.

Fish was an important part of people's diet in ancient China. **Archaeologists** have found pictures and models of fish. This model is probably from the Han **dynasty** and shows that fish was still popular at that time.

Cooking a meal

Ancient Chinese people cooked on box-shaped clay stoves. Fuel was pushed through a hole at one end of the stove to feed the fire inside. When the clay was hot, the food was put in cooking pots that fitted on top of the stove. Some of their food was cooked in saucepans on the stove. Other times their food was steamed.

Eating a meal

Ancient Chinese people ate their food from bowls. They used pottery bowls for every day and **lacquerware** bowls for special occasions. Their food was cut up into small pieces before it was cooked. People did not need knives or forks to eat with, instead they used chopsticks made from wood or ivory.

This patterned lacquerware bowl was found in a tomb in south central China. It was made during the Han dynasty and was probably used to serve food.

25

Clothes and Appearance

Clothes for rich people

Rich men and women in ancient China wore long silk robes tied with a sash or belt at the waist. Women had very elaborate hairstyles held in place with long pins or other jewelry. Men wore hats. They wore silk or fine leather shoes and boots. In winter, they wore thicker silk robes and furs.

The Da family

Archaeologists excavated three tombs at Mawangdui in south central China. The tombs belonged to the Da family who lived during the Han **dynasty.** In one tomb was the body of the wife of the prime minister of the Changsa **province.** He had been very rich and his wife had a lot of clothes. She probably had more clothes than someone from a **noble** family at that time. She was wearing twenty layers of clothes when she was buried. Her skirts and robes were made from silk. Some of them were colored with dyes made from plants and others had patterns painted or embroidered on them. More clothes were found in other parts of the tomb. Archaeologists also found flat-heeled shoes, socks, and gloves, all made from silk.

This piece of silk cloth was made around 551 C.E. Silk was often **traded** in exchange for goods and services.

This pair of silk shoes is 11.4 inches (29 centimeters) long. The shoe size shows they were made before footbinding began in the Song dynasty.

Clothes for poor people

Only rich and noble people wore silk and furs. Everyone else wore clothes made of cheaper fabric. They made fabric from fibers found in the stems of plants, like **hemp** and grass. Poor people worked hard and needed sensible clothes. Both men and women wore short tunics, tied at the waist and knee-length pants. On cold days, they wore sheepskins.

These farmers are wearing tunics and pants appropriate for farm work. Their sandals were probably made from straw or marsh plants.

Faiths and Beliefs

People in ancient China had several different faiths and beliefs. No one was forced to follow any one faith.

Confucius and Confucianism

Confucius, born in 551 B.C.E., was China's most famous scholar, teacher, and thinker. He believed that everyone had his or her place in society and should be content with it. They should obey their parents and rulers. People, Confucius said, were born good and had a duty to care for each other. He believed that sincerity, courage, knowledge, and sympathy were important. Everyone, from the **emperor** to the poorest **peasant,** should try to live in peace with the world around them. This set of beliefs is known as Confucianism.

The Chinese believed that there were two great natural forces in the world. They called these forces yin and yang. Each force had to balance the other exactly. Each force stood for things that were equal, but opposite. The Chinese thought yin and yang together explained everything that happened in the world.

Lao tzu and Taoism

No one knows whether Lao tzu really existed. He was supposed to have written down the ideas of Taoism. "Tao" means "the Way" and it refers to the way everything in nature works together. People, animals, plants, sky, and earth are all part of nature. If people follow the Way, and work together with everything in nature, they will find health, wealth, happiness, and long life.

By 700 C.E., there were more than 300,000 Chinese Buddhist **monks** and many temples and shrines, like this one, had been built.

Buddha and Buddhism

In about 100 C.E., **merchants** brought Buddhism to China from India. Buddhists believe that people live more than once. In each lifetime, they try to lead a better life than in the one before, until they do not need to be born again. At that point, they have reached Nirvana, or heaven.

The importance of ancestors

All people in ancient China respected their **ancestors.** They did not forget them when they died. In the Zhou **dynasty,** people built **temples** where they could remember their ancestors. Later, Chinese families put up wooden boards in their homes with their ancestors' names on them.

Death and Funerals

The ancient Chinese people believed that there was life after death.

Ancestors

People believed that their **ancestors** were still part of their living family. They told their ancestors family news and asked their advice on important family matters. On special festival days, they gave gifts of food to their ancestors.

Burials

Burying a dead body in the right place was very important. Chinese people always first asked the spirits of a place about the burial. They believed that there were spirits everywhere. If the spirits were happy with the burial place, good luck would come to the family of the dead person.

Living forever

Many Chinese people believed they would live forever, if only magicians could make the right magic drink. They called this magic drink the **Elixir of Life.** Many people tried to make it. Some used poisons, like mercury, and ended up killing those who drank it!

Princess Dou Wan was buried in this suit. It is made from 2,160 wafer-thin pieces of **jade** fastened with gold, silver, and **bronze** threads. Jade was used because people thought It would preserve the body.

The graves of poor people

Poor people were buried in simple graves when they died. They were buried with as many of their belongings as their family could spare. People believed they would need these things in their next life.

The tombs of the rich

Rich people could afford to bury more personal belongings with the dead. The dead person was dressed in fine silk clothes and put in several decorated coffins, one inside the other. The coffins were buried in a special underground tomb with the dead person's clothes, food, drink, lamps, ornaments made of bronze, jade, or **lacquerware,** and cooking pots. Pictures of everyday life were often carved or painted on the tomb walls. Between 3,000 and 4,000 years ago, very rich people had their servants and animals killed and buried with them. However, from the Qin **dynasty** onwards, models of people and animals were buried instead of the real ones.

In ancient China, models of acrobats and dancers were often put in graves. This model of a dancer was found in a Tang dynasty tomb.

Festivals and Fun

Festivals

In ancient China, people enjoyed music, dancing, and juggling at various festivals. The most important festival was the New Year festival that marked the start of the farming year. There were processions, kite-flying, and feasting. After the Tang **dynasty,** when the Chinese invented gunpowder, there were fireworks, too.

How do we know?

Models of dancers, acrobats, jugglers, and musicians were buried in the tombs of rich people in ancient China. Pictures of women dancing were painted on silk, **bamboo,** and paper. A book, *The Spring and Summer Annals,* written between 722 and 481 B.C.E., tells us that people in villages danced to celebrate good harvests and healthy animals on their farms.

The **inscriptions** on these **bronze** bells read that they once belonged to the Marquis of Ts'ai. He lived about 2,500 years ago. Each bell makes a different note when hit with a wooden hammer.

This is part of a modern Chinese New Year celebration. Everyone becomes a year older at New Year. Although birthdays are celebrated, everyone counts their age by the number of New Years they have seen.

Hunting

Poor people hunted animals for food. Pictures on tomb walls tell us that rich people hunted animals for fun. During the Shang dynasty, young **noblemen** hunted deer, wild boars, and hares from chariots driven by servants. The noblemen threw spears at the animals. Later, they hunted on horseback and used bows and arrows.

Gambling and board games

Gambling seems to have been popular in ancient China. Rich and poor people gambled. They gambled on the results of games of chance, on horse and dog races, and on cockfights. Rich people also had plenty of time to play board games similar to chess.

Roads

There were five different types of roads in ancient China about 2,700 years ago:
- pathways for people and animals;
- narrow roads for carts with wheels;
- wider roads for other vehicles;
- roads wide enough for two vehicles to travel side-by-side; and
- roads wide enough for three vehicles to travel side-by-side and pass each other.

The first **emperor,** Qin Shi Huangdi, wanted his orders to get to every corner of his **empire** quickly. He forced thousands of people to build "imperial roads." These roads were so wide that the middle lane was used only by the emperor and his messengers.

People as well as goods were carried in oxcarts. Oxcarts were slow, but they could carry very heavy loads. This model was found in a tomb from the Han **dynasty.** It is about 2,000 years old.

Bridges

Many roads had to cross rivers. If the banks were low, a stone or wooden bridge was built across the river.

If the banks were steep, the bridges were hung or suspended from strong **bamboo** poles. About 500 years later, during the Sui dynasty, the Chinese made wrought iron chains and built iron **suspension bridges.**

Water transportation

About 2,200 years ago, the ancient Chinese began to build canals. Canals made it easier to transport goods to markets. This meant that **trade** increased and people with goods to sell became richer. Rich people paid more taxes, which helped to pay for more roads, canals, and bridges.

The Grand Canal was built between 605 and 618 C.E. along an earlier canal. It joined the Yangtze (now Chang) River in the south to the Huai and Yellow Rivers in the north. The canal was soon busy with boats carrying goods.

Merchants and Trade

Money

At first, people in ancient China used cowrie shells as money. Later, some Chinese states used **bronze** coins shaped like these shells. Other bronze coins were shaped like spades and hoes. When Qin Shi Huangdi became **emperor** in 221 B.C.E., he decided that the **empire** should have only one set of coins. They were small, round, and bronze with a hole in the middle. They could be threaded on a string to carry around and saved bronze.

Merchants

At first, **merchants** were regarded as the lowest class in Chinese society. They were not allowed to wear silk, ride on horses, or become government officials. Emperors were afraid merchants would become too powerful. They tried to control them by making them the lowest class of all. Eventually, merchants were finally accepted into Chinese society and their sons could become government officials.

Government controls

About 3,000 years ago, Chinese rulers depended on **trading** to exchange goods for horses with which to fight their enemies.

This coin is shaped like a spade. It was made in about 550 B.C.E. The later round coins were known as "cash." When the long strings of cash became too heavy to carry, they began to be left behind for safety. Instead, people gave merchants a paper note in exchange. This was the start of paper money in China.

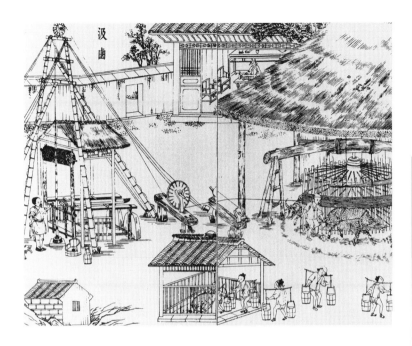

This woodcut shows salt being mined from the ground in southern China.

Chinese rulers also controlled salt and iron production. The state kept all the profits. The government collected taxes on goods along trade routes and in markets.

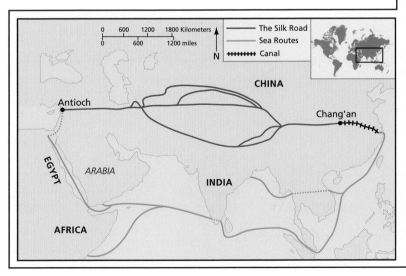

The silk trade

Silk from China was being traded in the Roman Empire about 2,000 years ago. Silk traders traveled mainly along the Silk Road. This was a series of well-known tracks from deep in China to Antioch (in modern Turkey). Each merchant carried his goods on camels from one city to the next. There, the goods were sold or exchanged for other merchandise. The merchant would then return to the first city to sell those goods. Silk also traveled from China to India, Arabia, Egypt, and other parts of Africa by a sea route.

The Engineers

The Chinese built some of the greatest engineering works of the ancient world.

Who was involved?

The **emperor** gave the orders. Army generals and top civil servants were in charge of the building projects. Engineers designed and built walls, roads, canals, palaces, and tombs. They also worked on **irrigation** and drainage projects to help farmers. The actual building was usually done by convicts and prisoners of war.

Canals

In China, the main rivers flow from west to east. But in ancient China, people and goods needed to move from south to north. So, Chinese engineers built canals to link the rivers by inland routes.

The Great Wall

The ancient Chinese built guard walls in north China. These were to protect the Chinese people from their enemies to the north and to protect them from each other. The first emperor, Qin Shi Huangdi, ordered that all the separate walls should be joined together and extended. This made one Great Wall, 4,161 miles (6,700 kilometers) long, to guard China's northern frontier. The Great Wall had watchtowers. Chinese soldiers could fire down at their enemies from the watchtowers. They also used the towers to signal warnings along the wall.

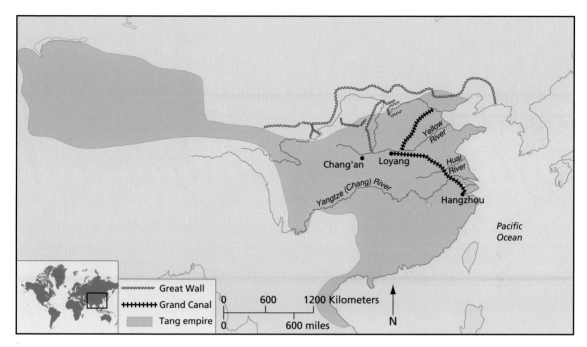

Chang'an • Loyang

Yellow River

Huai River

Yangtze (Chang) River

Hangzhou

Pacific Ocean

Great Wall
Grand Canal
Tang empire

| 0 | 600 | 1200 Kilometers |
| 0 | 600 miles | |

N

Controlling water

Engineers built dams and artificial islands to control the water flow in rivers and thus prevent drought or floods.

This map shows the Great Wall of China and the Grand Canal during the Tang **dynasty** (618–907 C.E.).

These people are building a dyke to hold back the waters of a river, which is going to flood. The long bundles of brushwood will trap the soil and loose pebbles. They will strengthen the bank against the water.

The Inventors

Lifting, measuring, and pulling

The first wheelbarrows were invented in ancient China. That meant people could push loads of up to 221 pounds (100 kilograms). Waterwheels were also invented in China. They raised water from rivers to **irrigate** the fields. Horse collars were another Chinese invention. They rested on a horses' chest muscles and not their throats. A horse could now pull a load without strangling itself. The odometer was invented to measure the distance traveled by a wheeled vehicle. No one knows who first created these inventions.

Gunpowder was probably discovered accidentally. The ancient Chinese used gunpowder to shoot arrows and to frighten their enemies with noise and smoke. They also used gunpowder to make fireworks.

Papermaking and printing

Like many other inventions, paper was not the idea of any one person. In ancient China, paper was first made from mashed silk fibers and was very expensive. Then, in about 105 C.E., a man named Cai Lun mashed plants and rags with water then pressed them together to make sheets of paper. This paper was cheaper than silk paper.

By 700 C.E., the Chinese were using wooden blocks to print books quickly and cheaply. These extra copies meant that knowledge could spread further.

Compasses and counting

By 1180 c.e., Chinese sailors were using a special ships' compass. The compass meant they could sail for long distances. Other scientists were interested in studying the stars, planets, and measuring time. Chinese scientists were good at arithmetic and used a calculator, called an **abacus.**

This is a page from a sacred Buddhist scroll called the *Diamond Sutra.* It was printed in 868 c.e. and is the oldest printed text in the world. It is also the first text to have a printed date.

Writing and Painting

Writing in pictograms

Chinese writing first appeared on **oracle** bones over 3,000 years ago. The people in ancient China used small drawings, called **pictograms,** as words. This worked well for words like "dog" and "tree," but it was much more difficult for words like "love," "hate," and "truth." People put two or three pictograms together when they wanted to write a difficult word.

One system of writing

At first, people in different parts of China used different pictograms for the same words. In about 221 B.C.E., **Emperor** Qin Shi Huangdi wanted everyone in his **empire** to be able to understand his orders in the same way. His close adviser, Li Si, wrote a list of 3,000 characters that were in use at the time. Everyone had to use the same pictograms. Chinese people still use the same system today.

Yin and Yang

Chinese artists wanted to keep yin and yang in balance in their pictures, as they were in real life. So they would balance a yin tortoise, earth, winter, or darkness with a yang dragon, sky, summer, or lightness. Artists did not paint exactly what they saw. They painted what they remembered, trying to capture the spirit of a place.

This picture was painted by Emperor Huizong in the 1100s. It shows a group of scholars meeting in a garden. Scholars, artists, poets, and emperors all enjoyed writing, painting, and good conversation.

Writing as art

In China, writing has always been a form of art, as well as a means of communication. People in ancient China wrote with ink brushes using careful strokes. Painting developed from this method of writing. In many silk scrolls, the writing is as important as the picture.

Chinese artists often painted mountains and water. If they painted people, they were very small and not important.

Chinese paintings

Some of the earliest paintings to survive were painted on the walls of tombs during the Han **dynasty.** Later, people in ancient China painted on silk, paper, and **bamboo.** They painted pictures of busy streets, landscapes, and court life.

43

Pottery and Porcelain

Making pottery

About 8,000 years ago, the Chinese made their first pots by smearing clay inside wooden bowls and baskets. When the clay was dry, it was baked in a fire to make it hard. Later, they made pots by coiling long strips of clay on top of each other. By 3000 B.C.E., the Chinese were using potters' wheels to make their pots.

Glazing pottery

The first pottery was rough to the touch and had a dull finish. During the Zhou **dynasty** (1122–221 B.C.E.), Chinese potters began painting their pots with glazes that became hard and shiny when the pot was fired. They added minerals to the glazes to make different colors.

This pottery animal was made around 2000 B.C.E. It was probably used as a jug, since liquid can be poured from its mouth.

Porcelain

The ancient Chinese discovered how to make **porcelain** about 1,300 years ago. The earliest porcelain was found in a Tang dynasty tomb, dated 661 C.E. Porcelain is harder and finer than pottery. Light is able to shine through it.

Archaeologists found model horses in the tomb of a Tang dynasty princess. These models were made of pottery and glazed in three colors. When the pottery was fired, the glazes mixed together to form new colors.

Making porcelain

To make porcelain, potters mixed fine white china clay, called **kaolin,** with the minerals feldspar and quartz. They added water to make a stiff paste that they shaped into bowls and figures. These were glazed and fired at very high temperatures. The feldspar melted around the clay, making a glassy surface. If the clay was thin, it made fine, delicate porcelain. If the clay was thick, it made strong, heat-resistant porcelain.

Porcelain was used throughout ancient China and exported to other countries. Rich people collected special pieces, but the best pieces were kept for the **emperor.**

A Chinese potter made this porcelain model during the Song dynasty. Chinese potters probably never left their country, yet their work was well known around the world.

Crafts and Metalwork

People in ancient China were very skilled craftworkers. They produced beautiful objects from many different materials.

Jade

Jade comes in colors from white to yellowish-brown. The Chinese preferred green and white jade. At first, Chinese craftworkers made jade into axes and knife blades. Then, during the Shang **dynasty,** metal replaced stone for making tools. Craftworkers began carving jade into jewelry and ornaments. Some of the finest carvings in ancient China were made of jade.

Bronze

Bronze is a mixture of copper, tin, and lead. The ancient Chinese first made bronze 3,000 years ago during the Shang dynasty.

People in ancient China made bronze objects by first making a clay mold. The mold was then filled with hot, liquid bronze. When the bronze cooled, they carefully took the clay mold apart so it could be used again.

This bronze monster mask and ring was made during the time of the first **emperor**. It was made using the lost wax method. A model would have been made of wax, with any decorations cut into it. Then, the wax model would be covered in clay to make a mold. A hole was left in the top of the mold. After the clay hardened, hot metal was poured into the hole. This melted the wax, which ran out of the mold as it was replaced by metal.

Iron

The Chinese began working with iron in about 450 B.C.E. They probably learned about iron from the west, where it had been made for over 1,000 years. The Chinese used iron to make their wooden tools, like **plough-shares** and drills, stronger. Stronger tools meant that more land could be **cultivated** and more salt could be mined. They also made iron cooking pots and weapons to replace bronze ones.

Lacquerware

People in ancient China decorated many objects, like trays, boxes, musical instruments, and models, with **lacquer.** They made lacquer from the sticky gray sap of the lacquer tree. They heated this sap with oil, which turned it black. Several coats of lacquer were painted on wooden and other objects. Each coat took many hours to dry. Sometimes they colored laquer with red, gold, and silver. When the lacquer dried hard, craftworkers polished it until it was as shiny as glass.

Archaeologists found this lacquer stag in a tomb in southern China. The stag had been buried for about 2,400 years when they **excavated** it in 1978. Lacquer can survive in damp conditions, so there are many objects from this period.

Silk Production

Clues from the past

The oldest piece of woven silk cloth ever found in China was made in about 2700 B.C.E. This was probably not the first silk ever made in China. **Archaeologists** have found small stone ornaments, dating from about 4000 B.C.E., that look like silkworms. The characters for "silk" and "silkworm" were written on **oracle** bones about 2,500 years later.

The legend of silk

There are many different stories about how the Chinese learned to make silk thread. One story tells how Hsi Ling Shi, wife of King Huang Ti, discovered silk around 2700 B.C.E. The king complained after he discovered that something was eating the leaves of his mulberry trees.

This is part of a picture painted on silk in the 1100s. For hundreds of years, the Chinese kept the way they made silk a secret. The punishment for telling the secret to foreigners was death.

His gardeners found that little caterpillars were to blame. Their cocoons fascinated Hsi Ling Shi. She accidentally dropped one into a bowl of hot water. Before she could get it out, a fine thread started to unwind from it. That thread was silk.

Raising silkworms

After silk was discovered, the Chinese began to raise silkworms. They let some cocoons hatch into moths. The silkworm farmers kept the moths in special warm houses where they controlled the light and air. The moths mated and produced eggs. When the silkworms hatched, they lived on **bamboo** trays and were fed mulberry leaves. Once they spun cocoons, some were allowed to turn into moths. Most of the cocoons were put into boiling water so that the silk fibers could be unwound.

Making silk cloth

Silk fibers were twisted together to make silk thread. The Chinese wove silk thread into cloth by hand, using looms. They wove the silk into different types of cloth, from fine gauze to heavy **brocade.**

Some silk cloth was embroidered, like this piece from the Tang **dynasty.** Silk was also made into clothes, flags, banners, and scrolls.

The Shang Dynasty

The Shang **dynasty** came to power around 1500 B.C.E. **Oracle** bones with the names of thirteen Shang kings scratched on them were found at Anyang, in north China. In 1923, **archaeologists** started **excavating** at Anyang. Later, they were able to create a picture of life In Shang times.

This **bronze** ax head would have been a useful weapon or tool. It may have been used in the many wars during the Shang dynasty.

The Shang rulers

The Shang kings often went to war against their enemies. They used slaves in their armies, as well as men provided by lords and landowners. The kings also used slaves to work their lands and do other jobs. These slaves were treated very badly. The Shang kings made human and animal **sacrifices** to

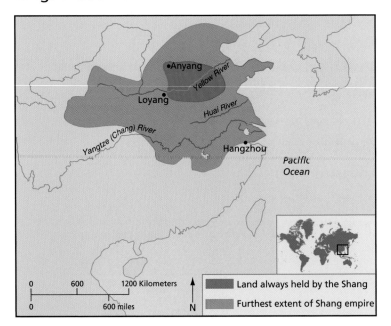

This map shows China during the Shang dynasty, 1500–1100 B.C.E.

their **ancestors.** When a Shang king or **noble** died, some of his slaves were killed and buried with him so they could look after him in the next life.

Life under the Shang rulers

Most ordinary Chinese people lived on the land, although some lived in towns. Craftworkers, who made bronze tools, weapons, bowls, and ceremonial cups, began to live near each other. Gradually, these communities grew into towns and cities, like Anyang. Craftworkers began making beautiful objects from **jade,** gold, and stone, as well as bronze. Chinese writing developed during the Shang dynasty, too.

The end of the Shang dynasty

Wars and rebellions weakened the Shang dynasty. Even the slaves rebelled against their harsh treatment. Around 1100 B.C.E., the Zhou army attacked Anyang. Many slaves left the Shang army and joined the Zhou. The Zhou won and a new dynasty came to power.

The Shang kings had many nature gods. The kings believed that ceremonies and sacrifices would bring good harvests. Bronze vessels were used to hold wine and food during these ceremonies. This bronze jar was probably used to warm the wine for a ceremony.

The Zhou Dynasty

The Zhou **dynasty** lasted for more than 900 years, from 1122 to 221 B.C.E. It is usually divided into two separate periods: the Western Zhou period (1122–770 B.C.E.) and the Eastern Zhou period (770–221 B.C.E.). The Eastern period was further divided into two periods: the Spring and Autumn period and the Warring States period.

The Western Zhou

The first part of the dynasty had its capital at Hao in western China. The Zhou kings believed they were descended from an agricultural god called the **Millet** Ruler.

This is part of a chariot decorated with silver designs. A Zhou craftworker made it during the Warring States period.

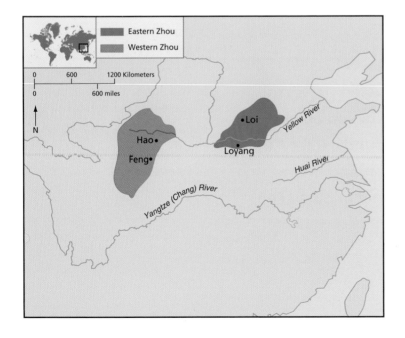

This map shows the lands of the Zhou dynasty and its capital cities (1122–221 B.C.E.).

Most Zhou people were farmers who grew crops. But in the land to the north, where it was too dry to grow crops, the people were **nomads.** The Zhou people saw them as **barbarians.** In 770 B.C.E., these nomads invaded the Zhou capital of Hao and killed the king.

Eastern Zhou: the Spring and Autumn period

The Zhou state prospered between 770 and 476 B.C.E. The **nobles** who owned land grew richer. They became more powerful and began to fight amongst themselves.

Eastern Zhou: the Warring States period

This period lasted from 476 to 221 B.C.E. It began with about 200 small states fighting each other. Ordinary people had to pay taxes to pay the soldiers. They lost much of their crops, which were either stolen or trampled by the armies. Eventually, as small states were defeated and taken over, seven large states formed, each ruled by a duke. By 221 B.C.E., Qin Shi Huangdi controlled all the states and ended the Zhou dynasty and the **feudal system.**

In about 250 B.C.E., Li Bing, an engineer and official, worked out a system of canals for controlling the waters of the Min River in western China. Before this, people thought floods were caused by a bad-tempered **emperor.** They soon found out the floods were caused by melting snow. The Dujiangyan canal system is one of the greatest engineering works in the world.

Empires and Kingdoms

The first empire

Qin Shi Huangdi became the first **emperor** of China in 221 B.C.E. He believed that all people were bad and had to be forced to obey him and his laws. So punishments for breaking the law were very harsh.

This is a Qin dynasty tally, shaped like a tiger. It is in two halves. One half stayed with the emperor and the other half with the army commander. The army could only fight when the two halves were put together. In this way the emperor tried to make certain that the army obeyed his orders.

The first peasant revolt

Qin Shi Huangdi's son became emperor in 210 B.C.E. He was harsh like his father, but weak and greedy as well. He ordered more and more **peasants** to fight on the frontiers of the **empire.** Eventually, a peasant army rose up against him. That army was defeated, but others soon followed. In 206 B.C.E. the Qin **dynasty** was defeated, and the Han dynasty came to power.

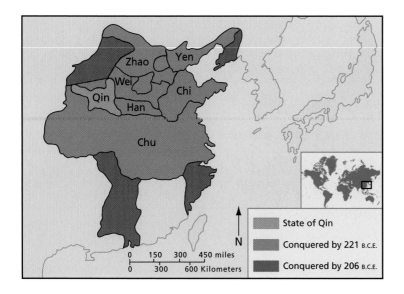

The Qin empire lasted from 221 to 206 B.C.E.

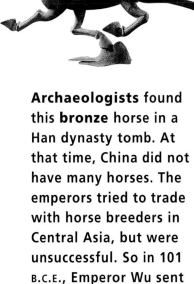

The Han dynasty

The Han emperors held the empire together and added new lands to it. **Trade** in silk, **jade,** and spices flourished. Ideas were carried from other lands and by 65 C.E. **merchants** and **monks** had brought the Buddhist religion to China. There were many rebellions by **noblemen** and peasants. **Nomads** raided northern China. In 220 C.E., the Han dynasty was overthrown and the empire collapsed.

Archaeologists found this **bronze** horse in a Han dynasty tomb. At that time, China did not have many horses. The emperors tried to trade with horse breeders in Central Asia, but were unsuccessful. So in 101 B.C.E., Emperor Wu sent an army and defeated the people. The army took the horses the emperor wanted.

The three kingdoms

China was then divided into three kingdoms: Wei in the north, Shu in the west, and Wu in the south and east. It was a hard time for everyone. Nomads from the north attacked. They were defeated in 383 C.E., but China was divided again. This time there were two main areas of power, one in the north and one in the south.

The Northern and Southern dynasties

The invaders from the north adopted Chinese ways of life. Meanwhile, the people who fled to the south brought their Chinese ways with them. In this way, China remained united in **culture.** Even so, there was a lot of fighting and rebellions. In 581 C.E. a new dynasty came to power.

China Reunited

The Sui dynasty: Wen Ti

In 581 C.E., Wen Ti founded the Sui **dynasty** after seizing the throne of the Northern kingdom. He sent an army to conquer south China and unite the whole country again. China was reunited for the first time since the Han dynasty in 220 C.E.

The Sui dynasty: Yang Ti

Yang Ti followed Wen Ti as **emperor.** He spent money on parks and palaces for himself, as well as for the Grand Canal. Yang Ti ordered people to pay taxes ten years in advance to cover the expenses. **Peasants** started to rebel and in 618 C.E. the army revolted and killed him.

This map shows China reunited, 581–1279 C.E.

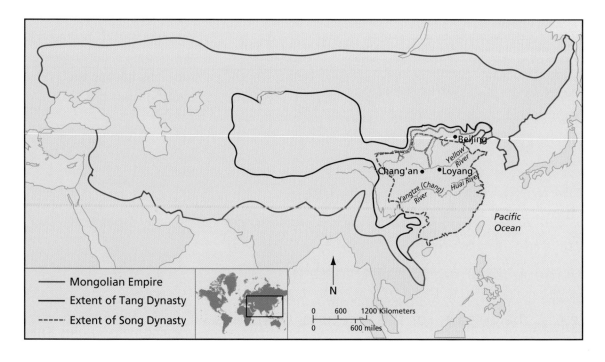

Mongolian Empire
Extent of Tang Dynasty
Extent of Song Dynasty

N

0   600   1200 Kilometers
0   600 miles

Beijing
Yellow River
Chang'an • • Loyang
Yangtze (Chang) River   Huai River
Pacific Ocean

The Tang dynasty

During this time, **porcelain** was invented and printing was developed. Painting became popular and the pictures that survived tell us a lot about everyday life. The Tang dynasty collapsed in 907 C.E.

Five Dynasties and Ten Kingdoms

After the Tang dynasty ended, five emperors over 53 years tried to reunite China. None succeeded until the first Song emperor in 978–79 C.E.

The Song dynasty

The first Song emperor reunited China and brought peace to his people. The north of the **empire** was still threatened by invaders. In 1126 C.E., the Song dynasty lost control of northern China. The emperor and his family were captured, but one son escaped. He fled south to Hangzhou and set up a new empire.

The Mongol invasion

By the 1220s, the Mongols from the north, led by Genghis Khan, conquered all of northern China. In 1279 C.E. the Mongols conquered the rest of the empire. For the first time, China was ruled by emperors who were not Chinese. The Mongols kept the Chinese way of life.

These two pottery models of Tang princesses tell us a lot about the clothes **nobles** wore.

This is Kublai Khan, the first non-Chinese emperor to rule China. He was the grandson of Genghis Khan. Kublai Khan ruled China from 1279 to 1294 C.E.

The Middle Kingdom

Zhong-guo

People in ancient China called their country Zhong-guo, "the Middle Kingdom," for two reasons. China was cut off from the rest of the world by mountains, seas, and deserts. People believed China was the center of the world because of these natural barriers. The second reason was that Chinese **culture** was ahead of the rest of the world. China influenced surrounding countries. Invaders adopted the Chinese way of life, rather than the other way around.

Keeping things the same

Although there were many rebellions and changes of **dynasty,** the way of life for most people went on unchanged. **Emperors,** from whatever dynasty, ruled. Well-educated officials

Natural barriers, like high mountains, helped make China feel cut off from the world. Even today, there are few roads through these mountains.

This is a Chinese style building in Japan. During the Tang dynasty, the Chinese set up cultural and trading links with Japan. The Chinese influenced building styles in Japan, but very little Japanese influence affected China.

ran the country. Agriculture was always more important than any other industry, even **trade.** Some foreign traders were allowed in to trade with Chinese **merchants,** but few Chinese merchants traveled outside of China. Those who did travel saw no reason to change their way of life. People's feelings of respect for their parents and **ancestors,** as well as their religion, probably added to their unwillingness to change.

This unwillingness to change was, until the fall of the Song dynasty in 1279 C.E., one of China's great strengths. Life was stable, in spite of rebellions. The emperor ruled from his palace and everyone else knew his or her place in life.

Time Line

B.C.E.

600,000 Early humans are living in parts of China.

500,000 Peking people live in caves at Zhoukoudian.

28,000 Early humans have been replaced by the true **ancestors** of man and are living at Zhoukoudian.

0 The caves at Xianrendong are occupied by hunter-gatherers.

6000 The first farmers start settling in the Yellow River valley.

5000 The village of Banpo is built in northern China.

4000 Stone models of silkworms are found from this date.

3500 Stone **plough-shares,** or hoes, are used in the Hangzhou Bay area. Fine painted pottery was made at Yangshao.

3000 Copper mining starts in China. Potters start making pottery on a wheel at Longshan.

2300 The date of the first **bronze** objects found and the earliest sample of woven silk.

1500 The start of the Shang **dynasty.**

1400 The first **oracle** bones are used.

1122 The Shang dynasty is replaced by the Zhou.

450 Iron working starts in China.

221 China becomes an **empire** under Qin Shi Huangdi.

210 Qin Shi Huangdi dies and is buried in a tomb with an army of terra-cotta soldiers.

206 The Han dynasty begins.

C.E.

65   Around this time, **merchants** and **monks** bring Buddhism to China from India.

100   Papermaking, using torn up silk, is invented.

150   A cheaper way of making paper is invented by Cai Lun.

581   The Sui dynasty, that reunites China, begins.

618   The start of the Tang dynasty.

661   The date of the earliest **porcelain** found so far.

700   Chinese invent printing by using carved wooden blocks.

907   The Tang dynasty ends and a period known as the Five Dynasties and Ten Kingdoms start.

960   The Song dynasty comes to power.

978-79   China is reunited under the Song dynasty.

1126   The Song lose control of northern China and the capital is moved to Hangzhou.

1180   The Chinese use a maritime compass for sea journeys to Arabia and Japan.

1279   The Mongols conquer all of China. Kublai Khan becomes for first non-Chinese person to rule over China.

The dynasties

Chinese history is divided into dynasties. Each dynasty is a period of time when one family was in power. The dynasties you have read about in this book are:

Shang	1500–1122 B.C.E.
Zhou	1122–221 B.C.E.
Qin	221–206 B.C.E.
Han	206 B.C.E.–220 C.E.

Three Kingdoms and Northern & Southern Dynasties period	220–580 C.E.
Sui	581–618 C.E.
Tang	618–907 C.E.

Five Dynasties & Ten Kingdoms period	907–960 C.E.
Song	960–1279 C.E.

Glossary

abacus counting frame with beads on wires

ancestor person from an earlier generation

archaeologist person who works out what happened in the past by studying old buildings and objects

artifact object made and used by someone in the past

bamboo type of giant grass with a hollow stem

barbarian ancient Chinese name for anyone who wasn't Chinese; an uncivilized person

brocade stiff silk material with raised patterns woven into it

bronze metal made from copper, tin, and lead

cultivate to prepare and use soil for growing crops

culture way of life

diviner person who sees the future or discovers hidden knowledge

dynasty ruling family; the period ruled by one particular family

Elixir of Life drink that was supposed to make a person live forever

emperor ruler of an empire

empire group of territories or people under one ruler

excavate to carefully dig up buried objects to find information about the past

fertile capable of growing large amounts of crops

feudal system system by which poorer people lived on richer people's land in exchange for some sort of service

flail tool for separating grain from straw

granary place where grain is stored after a harvest

hemp type of plant whose stem fibers can be woven into cloth

Homo sapiens scientific name for humans

inscription formal message made up of letters, numbers, or patterns cut into a solid surface

irrigate to water crops by channeling water from a river or lake along pipes or ditches; this process is called irrigation

jade hard stone used to make ornaments, jewelry, or tools

kaolin fine white clay from which porcelain is made

lacquer hard, glossy coating made from the sap of the lacquer tree; items made from lacquer are called lacquerware

mandate wish or command that has to be obeyed